ARDUINO PLAYS WITH DIGITAL AMMETER, VOLTMETER, POTENTIOMETER, MOTION DETECTOR AND SENSOR

Arduino plays with Digital Ammeter, Voltmeter, Potentiometer, Motion Detector and Sensor!!!

CONTENTS

ACKNOWLEDGMENTS

The writer might want to recognize the diligent work of the article group in assembling this book. He might likewise want to recognize the diligent work of the Raspberry Pi Foundation and the Arduino bunch for assembling items and networks that help to make the Internet of Things increasingly open to the overall population. Yahoo for the democratization of innovation!

INTRODUCTION

The Internet of Things (IOT) is a perplexing idea comprised of numerous PCs and numerous correspondence ways. Some IOT gadgets are associated with the Internet and some are most certainly not. Some IOT gadgets structure swarms that convey among themselves. Some are intended for a solitary reason, while some are increasingly universally useful PCs. This book is intended to demonstrate to you the IOT from the back to front. By structure IOT gadgets, the per user will comprehend the essential ideas and will almost certainly develop utilizing the rudiments to make his or her very own IOT applications. These included ventures will tell the per user the best way to assemble their very own IOT ventures and to develop the models appeared. The significance of Computer Security in IOT gadgets is additionally talked about and different systems for protecting the IOT from unapproved clients or programmers. The most significant takeaway from this book is in structure the tasks yourself.

ARDUINO BASED DIGITAL AMMETER

Ammeter is utilized to gauge current move through any heap or gadget. Here we will clarify about estimating of current by utilizing ohm's law. It will be very fascinating just as a decent use of essential science that we examined in our school days.

We all are outstanding of ohm's law, It expresses that

"the potential distinction between two posts or terminals of a conductor is legitimately relative to the measure of current go through a similar conductor" for steady of proportionality we use opposition, so here it comes the condition of ohm's law.

V = IR

- V = voltage over the conductor in Volt (v).

- I = current go through the conductor in Ampere (A).

- R = obstruction consistent of proportionality in Ohm (O).

So as to locate the present go through the gadget we simply rework the condition as beneath, or we can ascertain with ohm's law number cruncher.

I = V/R

So as to discover the current, we need a few information:

- Voltage

- Opposition

We are going to fabricate an arrangement obstruction alongside the gadget. As we have to discover voltage drop over the gadget, for that we need voltage readings when the voltage drop, that is conceivable in the obstruction in view of no extremity.

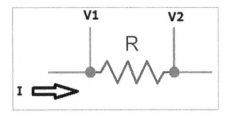

Like in the above chart, we need to locate the two voltages that are streaming over the resistor. The contrast between the voltages (V1-V2) at the two parts of the bargains us voltage drop over the resistor (R) and we isolate the voltage drop by the resistor esteem we get the present stream (I) through the gadget. That is the manner by which we can figure the Current worth going through it, how about we gets into it pragmatic execution.

Required Components:

- LCD 16x2.
- Resistor 22?.
- 10K pot.
- LED.
- Multimeter.
- Breadboard.
- Jumper cables.
- Arduino Uno.

Circuit Diagram and Connections:

The schematic outline of the Arduino Ammeter Project is pursues

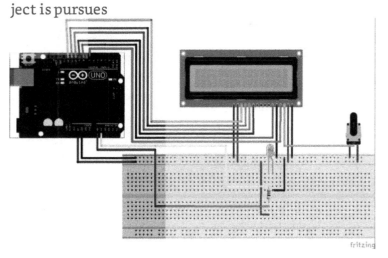

The schematic outline demonstrates the association of the Arduino Uno with LCD, resistor and LED. Arduino Uno is the power wellspring of the every single other part.

The Arduino has simple and advanced pins. The sensor circuit is associated with the simple contributions from which we get estimation of the voltage. The LCD is associate with the advanced pins (7,8,9,10,11,12).

The LCD has 16 sticks the initial two pins (VSS,VDD) and last two pins(Anode, Cathode) are associated with the gnd and 5v. The reset (RS) and empower (E) pins are associated with the Arduino advanced pins 7 and 8. The information pins D4-D7 are associated with the advanced pins of Arduino (9,10,11,12). The V0 stick is associated with the center stick of pot. The red and dark wires are 5v and gnd.

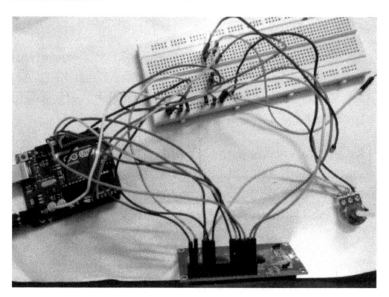

Current Sensing Circuit:

This Ammeter circuit comprises resistor and LED as burden. Resistor is associated in arrangement to the LED that present moves through the heap and voltage drops is resolved from the resistor. The terminal V1, V2 will associate with the simple contribution of the Arduino.

In the ADC of Arduino that coverts the voltage into 10 piece goals numbers from 0-1023. So we have to secret it in voltage worth utilizing the programming. Before that we have to know the insignificant voltage that ADC of Arduino can distinguish, that worth is 4.88mV. We duplicate the incentive from ADC with the 4.88mV and we get the genuine voltage into the ADC. Study the ADC of Arduino here.

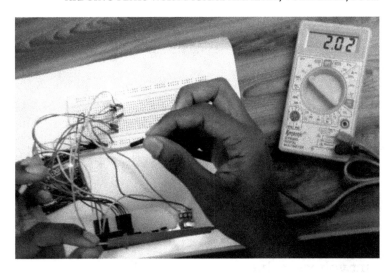

Calculations:

The voltage esteem from the ADC of Arduino is runs between 0-1023 and the reference voltage is extends between 0-5v.

For instance:

The estimation of the V1= 710, V2= 474 and R=22?, the contrast between the voltages are 236. We convert it into voltage by duplicate with 0.00488, at that point we get 1.15v. So the Voltage distinction is 1.15v, by isolating it by 22 here we get the present worth 0.005A. Here we have utilized the low worth 22ohm resistor as present sensor. This is the means by which we can quantify the present utilizing Arduino.

Arduino Code:

Complete code for arduino based ammeter to gauge current, is given toward the finish of this article.

Arduino writing computer programs is practically same as like c programming, first we proclaim the header documents. The header documents call the record in the capacity, as for the figuring I get the voltage esteems by utilizing analogread work.

```
int voltage_value0 = analogRead(A0);

int voltage_value1 = analogRead(A1);
```

A brief buoy variable is pronounced for holding voltage worth like buoy temp_val. The worth is increased with 0.00488 to get real voltage distinction then it is isolated by resistor incentive to locate the present stream. 0.00488v is the negligible voltage that the ADC of Arduino can distinguish.

```
int subraction_value =(voltage_value0 - voltage_value1);

float temp_val = (subraction_value*0.00488);

float current_value = (temp_val/22);
```

Code

```
#include<LiquidCrystal.h>
LiquidCrystal lcd (7,8,9,10,11,12);
void setup() {
// put your setup code here, to run once:
Serial.begin(9600);
lcd.begin(16,2);
lcd.clear();
}
void loop() {
// put your main code here, to run repeatedly:
int voltage_value0 = analogRead(A0);
int voltage_value1 = analogRead(A1);
  int subraction_value =(voltage_value0 - voltage_value1);
float temp_val = (subraction_value*0.00488);
float current_value = (temp_val/22);
Serial.print(current_value);
lcd.setCursor(0,0);
lcd.print("current value=");
lcd.setCursor(0,1);
lcd.print (current_value);
lcd.print("A");
delay(1000);
}
```

USING PYTHON WITH ARDUINO - CONTROLLING A LED

Arduino has consistently been an amazing and a simple to utilize getting the hang of/creating stage with regards to open source equipment improvement. In

the present current world, each equipment is controlled by an elevated level universally useful programming language to make it increasingly powerful
and easy to use. One such language is Python. Python
is a deciphered, object-arranged, significant level
programming language with dynamic semantics
with elevated level inherent information structures,
joined with dynamic composing as well as dynamic
authoritative, make it alluring for Rapid Application
Development.

Consolidating the intensity of Arduino and Python
will open ways to heaps of potential outcomes since
python has an expanded efficiency with its capacity
to connect with different stages like openCV, Matlab
and so forth.. So in this instructional exercise we will
figure out how we can introduce python on our PC
and how to utilize it with Arduino for flipping the on-
board LED of Arduino.

In this way, Let's get started....

Materials Required:

- Arduino Uno (or any Arduino Boards)
- Computer with Internet connection

Installing Python on your Computer:

Clearly the initial phase in this instructional exercise would introduce Python on our PC. The means referenced underneath are appropriate just for windows clients running either 32-piece or 64-piece OS. The establishment strategy for MAC and Linux is unique.

- Snap on 32-piece Python-2.7.9 and this will introduce the 32-piece Python IDLE on your Computer. Try not to download the 64-piece form or refreshed renditions since they don't offer help for our Arduino Libraries. Regardless of whether your Computer is working on 64-piece you can utilize 32-piece Python itself.

- Open the downloaded exe document and adhere to through the guidance. Try not to change the index wherein the python is getting introduced. It will be C:\Python27 of course and leave it in that capacity.

- While the establishment happens you may get an admonition from your enemy of infection (assuming any) all things considered snap on permit.

That is it!, python is effectively introduced on our PC. You can confirm it via looking for "Python IDLE" in Windows search box and opening it.

At the point when opened you ought to get the accompanying screen. This window is known as the Python Shell and we will allude to it as "Python shell" from now.

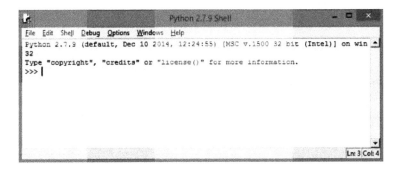

This screen is known as the Python Shell. You can legitimately code in here and get the yield on a similar screen or make another record and compose the program there and confirm the program here. We will later dive into the subtleties of making a python program, for the present let us check if python is working.

To do as such, essentially type "print (1+1)" and press enter. You should see the outcome getting printed as demonstrated as follows.

Getting PySerial in Python:

The following stage is to introduce pyserial. PySerial is a Python API module which is utilized to peruse and compose sequential information to Arduino or some other Microcontroller.

Snap on Pyserial Windows to download PySerial. The subsequent download will be an exe document which can be straightforwardly introduced. Try not to change any setting while at the mean time introducing. Leave it to the default registry and default settings.

Presently, let us check if PySerial is introduced appropriately. To do this, open Python Shell again and type in

import sequential. In case that the library was effectively introduced, at this point you ought not get any blunder messages as appeared in the image beneath.

This instructional exercise accept that you know about Arduino and have involvement in transferring activities to Arduino. So let us legitimately bounce into our Python program. On the off chance that you are a novice with Arduino check our Arduino Projects and start from LED Blinking with Arduino.

Our First Arduino Python Program:

As said before we will control the in-fabricated Arduino board LED utilizing Python content. Give us a chance to begin with the Arduino code.

Program for Arduino:

The total program for this Arduino python instructional exercise is given toward the finish of this page. Peruse further to know how it functions.

Inside the arrangement work we instate the sequential correspondence at 9600 baud rate and announce that we will utilize the inherent drove as yield and turn it low during project start. We have additionally sent an invite message to python by means of sequential print as demonstrated as follows:

```
void setup() {

  Serial.begin(9600); //initialize serial COM at 9600
baudrate

  pinMode(LED_BUILTIN, OUTPUT); //make the
LED pin (13) as output

  digitalWrite (LED_BUILTIN, LOW);

  Serial.println("Hi!, I am Arduino");

}
```

Inside the circle work, we read whatever the information that is coming in sequentially and doling out the incentive to the variable "information". Presently dependent on the estimation of this variable ("information") we flip the implicit drove as demonstrated as follows.

```
void loop() {

while (Serial.available()){

  data = Serial.read();

}

if (data == '1')

digitalWrite (LED_BUILTIN, HIGH);

else if (data == '0')

digitalWrite (LED_BUILTIN, LOW);

}
```

Program for Python:

The total python program for this instructional exercise is given toward the finish of this page. Peruse further to realize how to compose and utilize the equivalent.

- Open your Python Shell (Python IDLE) and

snap File->New

- This will open another content record where you can type in your program.

- Before we type anything lets spare the document, by Ctrl+S. Type in any name and snap on spare. This will consequently spare you document in ".py" augmentation.

- Presently, type in the program or glue the python code given toward the finish of this page. The clarification for the equivalent is given underneath lastly run the program.

In our program the initial step is import the sequential and time library. The sequential library as said before will be utilized to peruse and compose sequential information and the time library will be utilized to make delays in our program. These two libraries can be imported in our program utilizing the accompanying two lines:

```
import serial #Serial imported for Serial commu-
nication

import time #Required to use delay functions
```

The following stage is instate a sequential item utilizing our sequential library. In this program we have named our sequential article as "ArduinoSerial". In this line we have to specify the name of the COM port to which our Arduino is associated and at what baud rate it is working as demonstrated as follows.

```
ArduinoSerial = serial.Serial('com18',9600)
```

Note: It is essential to specify the right COM port name. It can found by utilizing the Device supervisor on your PC.

As soon the sequential item is introduced we should hold the program for two seconds for the Serial correspondence to be built up. This should be possible by utilizing the beneath line:

```
time.sleep(2)
```

Presently we can peruse or compose anything from/ to our Arduino Board.

The accompanying line will peruse anything originating from Arduino and will print it on the shell window

```
print ArduinoSerial.readline()
```

You can likewise dole out the incentive to a variable

and use it for calculations.

The accompanying line will compose the estimation of the parameter to Arduino Board.

```
ArduinoSerial.write('1')
```

This line will compose '1' to the Arduino. You can send anything from decimals to strings utilizing a similar line.

Presently, returning to our program, inside the endless while circle, we have the accompanying lines

```
var = raw_input() #get input from user

    print "you entered", var #print the input for con-
firmation

    if(var == '1'): #if the value is 1

        ArduinoSerial.write('1') #send 1

        print ("LED turned ON")

        time.sleep(1)

    if(var == '0'): #if the value is 0
```

```
ArduinoSerial.write('0') #send 0

print ("LED turned OFF")

time.sleep(1)
```

The line var=raw_input will get any worth that is composed in the Shell content and allocate that incentive to the variable var.

Afterward, if the worth is 1 it will print '1' sequentially to Arduino and if 0 it will print '0' sequentially to Arduino. The code in our Arduino Program (examined above) we will flip the LED dependent on the got worth.

When the total program is done your content should look something like this underneath

Presently click on Run - > Run Module or press F5 this may request that you spare the program and afterward will dispatch it.

Controlling LED with Python and Arduino:

The working of this venture is quite straight forward. Transfer the program to your Arduino and check it is associated with the equivalent COM port as referenced in the python program. At that point Launch the Python program as referenced previously.

This will dispatch a python shell content as demonstrated as follows. The window on the left is the shell window demonstrating the yield and the window on the privilege is the content demonstrating the program.

As should be obvious the string "Howdy!, I am Arduino" entered in the Arduino program is gotten by the Python and showed on its shell window.

At the point when the shell window requests to enter esteems, we can enter either 0 or 1. On the off chance that we send 1 the LED on the Arduino Board will turn ON and on the off chance that we send 0 the LED on our Arduino Board will mood killer. Demonstrating an effectively association between our Arduino Program and Python.

There are two program given beneath, one to be transferred and keep running from Arduino and second is to be kept running from Python Shell in Windows.

Expectation you comprehended the task and had the option to make it work. In our next task we will realize what else should be possible cool with Python and Arduino by investigating profound into other python modules like Vpython, gamepython and so forth. Up to that point stay tuned....

Code

Program for Arduino:

```
int data;
void setup() {
  Serial.begin(9600); //initialize serial COM at 9600 baudrate
  pinMode(LED_BUILTIN, OUTPUT); //make the LED pin (13) as output
  digitalWrite (LED_BUILTIN, LOW);


  Serial.println("Hi!, I am Arduino");
}


void loop() {
while (Serial.available()){
  data = Serial.read();
}
if (data == '1')
digitalWrite (LED_BUILTIN, HIGH);
else if (data == '0')
```

```
digitalWrite (LED_BUILTIN, LOW);
}
```

Python Program for Windows:

```
import serial #Serial imported for Serial communication
import time #Required to use delay functions


ArduinoSerial = serial.Serial('com18',9600) #Create Serial port object called arduinoSerialData
time.sleep(2) #wait for 2 secounds for the communication to get established
print ArduinoSerial.readline() #read the serial data and print it as line
print ("Enter 1 to turn ON LED and 0 to turn OFF LED")


while 1: #Do this forever
  var = raw_input() #get input from user
   print "you entered", var #print the intput for confirmation


  if(var == '1'): #if the value is 1
  ArduinoSerial.write('1') #send 1
  print ("LED turned ON")
  time.sleep(1)


  if(var == '0'): #if the value is 0
```

```
ArduinoSerial.write('0') #send 0
print ("LED turned OFF")
time.sleep(1)
```

DC-DC BUCK CONVERTER CIRCUIT - HOW TO STEP DOWN DC VOLTAGE

We are gonna to make a Buck Converter Circuit utilizing Arduino as well as N-Channel MOSFET with a greatest current limit of 6 amps. We are gonna to step down 12v DC to any an incentive somewhere in the range of 0 and 10v DC. We could control the yield voltage esteem by turning the potentiometer.

A buck converter is a DC to DC converter, which steps down DC voltage. It is much the same as a transformer with one contrast; though transformer steps down AC voltage buck converter steps down DC voltage. Effectiveness of buck converter is under a transformer.

Key parts of buck converter are mosfet; either n-channel or p-channel as well as high recurrence Square Pulse Generator (either a clock IC or microcontroller). Arduino is utilized here as Pulse Generator, a 555 Timer IC can likewise be utilized for this reason. Here we have shown this Buck converter by controlling DC-Motor speed with Potentiometer, likewise tried the voltage utilizing Multimeter.

Required Components:

- Arduino Uno
- IRF540N
- Inductor(100Uh)
- Capacitor (100uf)
- Schottky Diode
- Potentiometer
- 10k, 100ohm Resistor
- Load

- 12v Battery

Circuit Diagram and Connections:

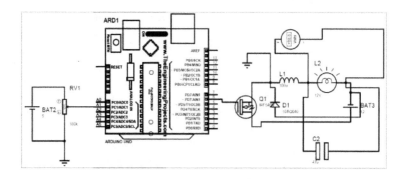

Make associations as appeared in circuit graph above for DC-DC Buck Converter.

- Associate one terminal of inductor to well-spring of mosfet, and another to LED in arrangement with 1k resistor. Burden is associated in parallel to this game plan.

- Associate 10k resistor among door and source.

- Associate capacitor in parallel to stack.

- Associate positive terminal of battery to deplete and negative to capacitor's negative terminal.

- Associate p terminal of diode to negative of

battery and n terminal straightforwardly to source.

- PWM stick of Arduino goes to door of mosfet

- GND stick of Arduino goes to wellspring of mosfet. Do interface it there or circuit won't work.

- Interface potentiometer's extraordinary terminals to 5v stick and GND stick of Arduino separately. While wiper terminal to simple stick A1.

Capacity of Arduino:

As of now clarified, Arduino sends clock heartbeats to base of MOSFET. Recurrence of these clock heartbeats is approx. 65 Khz. This causes extremely quick exchanging of mosfet and we get a normal voltage esteem. You ought to find out about ADC and PWM in Arduino, which will clear you how high recurrence heartbeats are produced by Arduino:

- Arduino Based LED Dimmer utilizing PWM

- How to Use ADC in Arduino Uno?

Capacity of MOSFET:

Mosfet is utilized for two purposes:

- For fast exchanging of the yield voltage.

- To give high current less dispersal of warmth.

Capacity of inductor:

Inductor is utilized to control voltage spikes which can harm mosfet. Inductor stores vitality when mosfet is on and discharges this put away vitality when mosfet is off. Since recurrence is high, estimation of inductance required for this intention is low (around 100uH).

Capacity of Schottky Diode:

Schottky diode finishes the circle of current when

mosfet is turned off and hence guaranteeing smooth stock of current to stack. Aside from this, schottky diode scatters exceptionally low warmth and work fine at higher recurrence than customary diodes.

Capacity of LED:

Brilliance of LED shows the progression down voltage crosswise over burden. As we pivot the Potentiometer, brilliance of LED fluctuates.

Capacity of potentiometer:

At the point when wiper terminal of potentiometer is lost to various position, voltage among it and ground changes which thusly changes the simple worth got by stick A1 of arduino. This new worth is then mapped somewhere in the range of 0 and 255 and afterward given to stick 6 of Arduino for PWM.

** Capacitor smooths out voltage given to stack.

Why resistor among door and source?

Indeed, even scarcest commotion at door of MOSFET can turn it on, thus to keep this from happening it is constantly encouraged to associate high esteem resistor among entryway and source.

Code Explanation:

Complete Arduino code, for producing high recurrence beats, is given in the code segment beneath.

Code is straightforward and clear as crystal, so here we have clarified just couple of parts of code.

Variable x is allocated the simple worth that is gotten from simple stick A0 of Arduino

```
x= analogRead(A1);
```

Variable w is doled out the mapped worth which is somewhere in the range of 0 and 255. Here the ADC estimations of Arduino are mapped to 2 to 255 utilizing guide work in Arduino.

```
w = map(x,0,1023,0,255);
```

Typical recurrence of PWM for stick 6 is approx. 1khz. This recurrence isn't appropriate for purposes like buck converter. Consequently this recurrence must be expanded to an elevated level. This can be accomplished utilizing a one line code in void arrangement:

```
TCCR0B = TCCR0B & B11111000 | B00000001;//
change frequency of pwm to 65 KHZ approx.
```

Working of DC-DC Buck Converter:

At the point when circuit is turned on, mosfet turns on and off with a recurrence of 65 khz. This makes inductor store vitality when mosfet is on and after that give this put away vitality to stack when mosfet switches off. Since this occurs at extremely high recurrence, we get a normal estimation of beat yield voltage relying upon the situation of wiper terminal of potentiometer as for 5v terminal. What's more, as this voltage between wiper terminal as well as ground increments so does the mapped an incentive on pwm stick no. 6 of Arduino.

Let's say this mapped value is 200. Then PWM voltage on pin 6 will be at:

[(200*5) / 255]= 3.921 volts

Furthermore, since MOSFET is a voltage subordinate gadget, this pwm voltage at last decides the voltage crosswise over burden.

Here we have shown this Buck converter by turning a DC-Motor and on Multimeter. We have controlled the speed of engine with Potentiometer and controlled the splendor of LED with Potentiometer.

Code

int x; // initialize variables

```
int w;
void setup() {
 pinMode(6,OUTPUT);// pwm pin 6 as output pin
 pinMode(A1,INPUT);// analog pin as input
  TCCR0B = TCCR0B & B11111000 | B00000001;//
change frequency of pwm to 65 KHZ approx( ex-
plained under code section)
 Serial.begin(9600);// begin serial communication
}
void loop() {
 x= analogRead(A1);
 w= map(x,0,1023,0,255);
 analogWrite(6,w); // write mapped value on pin 6
 Serial.print("w  "); //print mapped value on screen
 Serial.println(w);
}
```

❖ ❖ ❖

SIMPLE ARDUINO DIGITAL VOLTMETER

With a straightforward learning of Arduino as well

as Voltage Divider Circuit, we can transform the Arduino into Digital Voltmeter as well as can gauge the information voltage utilizing Arduino and a 16x2 LCD show.

Arduino has a few simple info sticks that interface with an ADC inside the Arduino. The Arduino ADC is a ten-piece converter, implies that the yield worth will run from 0 to 1023. We will acquire this incentive by utilizing the analogRead() work. In the event that you know the reference voltage you can undoubtedly compute the voltage present at the simple information. We can utilize voltage divider circuit to ascertain the information voltage. Get familiar with ADC in Arduino here.

The voltage estimated is shown on the 16x2 Liquid Crystal Display (LCD). We have likewise shown the voltage in Serial Monitor of Arduino IDE and affirmed the deliberate voltage utilizing Multimeter.

Hardware Required:

- Arduino uno

- 10 k ohm resistor

- breadboard

- 100 k ohm resistor

- jumper wires

- 16x2 LCD

- 10 k ohm potentiometer

Voltage Divider Circuit:

Before going into this Arduino Voltmeter circuit, lets talk about the Voltage Divider Circuit.

Voltage divider is a resistive circuit as well as appeared in figure. In this resistive system we have 2 resistors. As appeared in figure, R1 as well as R2 which are 10k as well as 100k ohm. The midpoint of branch is taken to estimation as an anolog contribution to the Arduino. The voltage drop crosswise over R2 is called Vout , that is the separated voltage of our circuit.

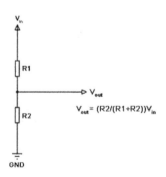

Formulae:

Utilizing the known worth (two resistor esteems R1,

ANBAZHAGAN K

R2, and the info voltage), we can substitute in the condition beneath to ascertain the yield voltage.

Vout = Vin (R2/R1+R2)

This condition expresses that the yield voltage is legitimately corresponding to the info voltage and the proportion of R1 as well as R2.

By applying this condition in the Arduino code the information voltage can be effectively determined. Arduino can just gauge the DC input voltage of +55v, as such, when estimating 55V, the Arduino simple stick will be at its greatest voltage of 5V so it is sheltered to quantify inside this farthest point. Here the resistors R2 as well as R1 worth is set to 100000 and 10000 for example in the proportion of 100:10.

Circuit Diagram and Connections:

Association for this Arduino Digital Voltmeter is basic and appeared in the circuit outline beneath:

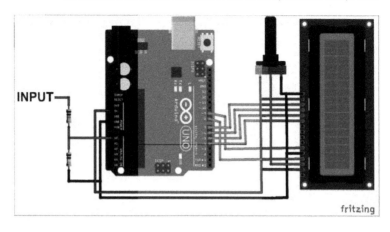

Stick DB4, DB5, DB6, DB7, RS and EN of LCD are straightforwardly conneted to Pin D4, D5, D6, D7, D8, D9 of Arduino Uno

The Center purpose of two resistors R1 as well as R2, which makes the voltage divider circuit, is associated with Arduino Pin A0. While the other 2 closures are associated with the info volt (voltage to be estimated) and gnd.

Coding Explanation:

Full Arduino code for estimating the DC voltage is given in the Code part underneath. Code is straightforward and can be effectively comprehended.

The primary piece of the code is to change over and map the given info voltage into showed yield voltage with the assistance of the above given condition Vout = Vin (R2/R1+R2). As referenced before Arduino ADC yield worth will extend from 0 to 1023 and the Arduino max yield voltage is 5v so we need to increase the simple contribution at A0 to 5/1024 to get the genuine voltage.

```
void loop()

{

  int analogvalue = analogRead(A0);

  temp = (analogvalue * 5.0) / 1024.0;      // FOR-
MULA USED TO CONVERT THE VOLTAGE

  input_volt = temp / (r2/(r1+r2));
```

Here we have shown the deliberate voltage esteem on LCD and sequential screen of Arduino. So here in the code Serial.println is utilized to print the qualities on Serial screen and lcd.print is utilized to print the qualities on 16x2 LCD.

```
Serial.print("v = ");        // prints the voltage value
in the serial monitor

  Serial.println(input_volt);

  lcd.setCursor(0, 1);
```

```
    lcd.print("Voltage= ");        // prints the voltage
 value in the LCD display

    lcd.print(input_voltage);
```

This is the manner by which we can undoubtedly figure the DC voltage utilizing Arduino. Its bit hard to compute the AC voltage utilizing Arduino, you can check the equivalent here.

Code

```
#include <LiquidCrystal.h>  // LIBRARY TO ACCESS
THE LCD DISPLAY
LiquidCrystal lcd( 4, 5, 6, 7,8 ,9 );
float input_volt = 0.0;
float temp=0.0;
float r1=10000.0;  //r1 value
float r2=100000.0;   //r2 value
void setup()
{
  Serial.begin(9600);   // opens serial port, sets data
rate to 9600 bps
  lcd.begin(16, 2);      //// set up the LCD's number of
columns and rows
  lcd.print("DC DIGI VOLTMETER");
}
void loop()
{
  int analogvalue = analogRead(A0);
  temp = (analogvalue * 5.0) / 1024.0;    // FORMULA
```

USED TO CONVERT THE VOLTAGE

```
  input_volt = temp / (r2/(r1+r2));
if (input_volt < 0.1)
  {
  input_volt=0.0;
  }
  Serial.print("v= ");          // prints the voltage value
in the serial monitor
  Serial.println(input_volt);
  lcd.setCursor(0, 1);
  lcd.print("Voltage= ");          // prints the voltage
value in the LCD display
  lcd.print(input_volt);
  delay(300);
}
```

DIY ARDUINO BASED CNC PLOTTER MACHINE

CNC Machines are utilized to draw anything or plan

any mechanical part as indicated by the structure program bolstered into their controller unit. Controller unit can be either PC or microcontroller. CNC machines have stepper as well as servo engines to draw the plan according to the fed program.

In the wake of looking into on CNC machines, I chose to construct my own CNC machine utilizing locally accessible materials. There are so a numerous CNC machines on the planet, some of which are a lot of specialized and complex to make or even work them appropriately. Consequently, I chose to make a CNC Plotter Machine dependent on Arduino which is by a wide margin the least complex to make.

This DIY Arduino CNC Machine can draw a wide portion of the fundamental shapes, messages and even kid's shows. It's activity is like the manner in which a human hand composes. It's quicker and progressively exact contrasted with the manner in which a person can compose or draw.

Operation of CNC Machine:

For a CNC plotting machine to work, 3 tomahawks are required (x-pivot, y-hub and z-hub. The x-hub and y-hub work as one to make a 2D picture on a plain paper. These x and y pivot are put 90 degrees to one another with the end goal that any point on the plain surface is characterized by a given estimation of x and y. The z-hub is utilized lift as well as lower the pen onto the plain paper.

Contingent upon the picture to be drawn, the PC will produce the suitable organizes and send them to the microcontroller through the USB port. The microcontroller translates these directions and after that controls the places of the engines to make the picture. Here we have utilized Arduino as the Microcontroller to fabricate this CNC Machine.

So we should begin assembling this gadget bit by bit.

What You Need:

Note: My structure is very unique in equipment as far as size and the materials utilized. I couldn't discover old DVD drives so I picked printer parts. Whichever you use, guarantee that it has a stepper engine.

Equipment Requirement:

- Aluminum sheet (710mm x 710mm)

- Old HP/Epson printer. You can utilize old PC DVD drives

- Fasteners and nuts

- Perspex glass

- Arduino UNO

- L293D engine driver shield

- Small scale servo engine

- A pen

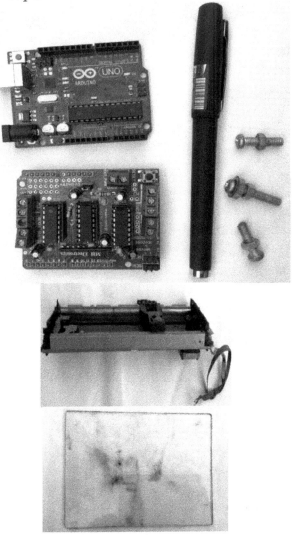

Devices:

- Screwdriver

- Drill

- Cutting device (hacksaw)

- Paste

- Seat gadget

Virtual products:

For the productive activity of this machine, the accompanying programming projects are utilized. Go to the different sites and download them.

- Arduino IDE rendition 1.6.6 or later forms from here

- Preparing IDE form 3.1.1 or later form from here

- Inkscape adaptation 0.48.5. Download it from here.

- Grbl controller (discretionary)

The Base for CNC Plotter Machine:

The primary body of this gadget is the base which supports all the significant pieces of the machine together with the goal that the machine is firm and is additionally convenient. In this structure we will utilize aluminum to develop the base since it is light, easy to twist and cut and furthermore it gives a decent glossy appearance since it doesn't rust.

The structure and measurements of my base is demonstrated as follows:

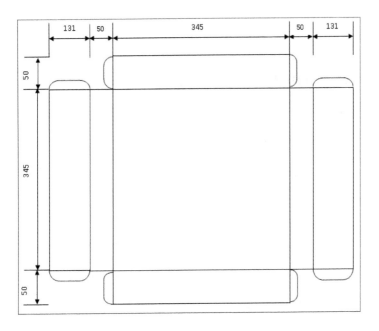

Note: All measurements are in millimeters.

After all the twisting and cutting, I had the option to deliver an extremely firm base as demonstrated as follows:

Assembly of the X, Y and Z Axes:

To make x and y tomahawks, two printer supports are utilized. Every one of these parts contains a stepper engine and a belt drive instrument ussually used to move the catridge forward and backward.

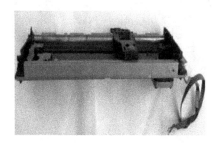

For the z-pivot, a small servo engine is connected on

the y-hub utilizing paste. This servo engine is utilized to move the pen here and there. A decent help component ought to be developed that will empower the free here and there development of the pen.

Drawing Platform for CNC Machine:

Because of the tremendous size of this machine, the gadget is equipped for drawing on an A5 measured paper. In this manner we will remove an A5 (148mmx210mm) estimated stage from the Perspex glass and after that stick it onto the x-hub moving part utilizing paste.

Wiring and Circuit of CNC Machine:

Addition the L293D engine driver shield onto the Arduino UNO board. This shield can drive two stepper engines simultaneously and two servo engines. Associate the two stepper engines as demonstrated as follows. The ground association ought to be left detached since the engines are bipoplar type.

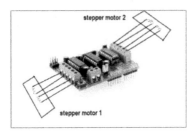

Additionally join the smaller than expected servo engine to servo1. Interface a 7.5V - 9V power stockpile to the power port of the engine driver shield. The machine is presently prepared for testing.

Arduino CNC Machine Code and Testing:

First we have to test the stepper engines and see whether they are associated effectively.

Since we are utilizing the L293D engine driver shield, we have to download the AFmotor Library from here. At that point include it into your Arduino IDE library envelope. Guarantee you rename it to AFMotor. In the event that the Arduino IDE was open close it and open it again and click on record - > models - > Adafruit Motor Shield Library - > stepper. Guarantee you pick the right port and board in apparatuses and after that transfer the code into the Arduino board. A few developments ought to be seen on stepper engine one.

So as to test engine two, change the engine port from

2 to 1 in the accompanying line and afterward transfer the code once more.

```
#include <AFMotor.h>

// Connect a stepper motor with 48 steps per revolution (7.5 degree)

// to motor port #2 (M3 and M4)

AF_Stepper motor(48, 2);
```

Arduino Code for CNC Machine:

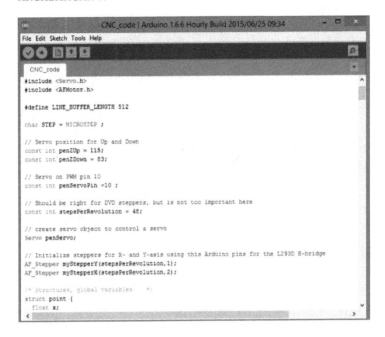

When the stepper engines are reacting properly, duplicate the Arduino code for CNC machine from the Code area underneath and transfer it to the Arduino board. You can download the code from here moreover.

G-Code for CNC Machine:

G - CODE is the language where we tell modernized machines (CNC) to accomplish something. It's fundamentally a document that contains X, Y as well as Z arranges.

For instance:

```
G17 G20 G90 G94 G54

G0 Z0.25X-0.5 Y0.

Z0.1

G01 Z0. F5.

G02 X0. Y0.5 I0.5 J0. F2.5

X0.5 Y0. I0. J-0.5

X0. Y-0.5 I-0.5 J0.

X-0.5 Y0. I0. J0.5

G01 Z0.1 F5.

G00 X0. Y0. Z0.25
```

Composing a G-Code for only a basic square can be truly testing however fortunately we have a product which can enable us to create a G-Code. This product is designated "Inkscape", download it from here.

You can produce your own G-Code utilizing Inkscape, which we have clarified in next area or however you can utilize promptly accessible G-Codes on the web.

Before I tell you the best way to create G-Codes utilizing Inkscape lets talk about on the most proficient method to send those G-Codes into the Arduino. The product that will empower us send G-Codes into the Arduino is called Processing.

Processing IDE to upload the G-Code:

This stage will enable us to send the G-Codes to the Arduino board. To do as such, you should install the GCTRL.PDE record.

Install GCTRL.pde record from here and open it utilizing Processing IDE

When you've opened it in the Processing IDE, click run. A window shows up with every one of the guidelines. Press p on the console. The framework will request that you pick a port. So select the port on which your Arduino board is associated. I my case it's port 6.

Presently press g and peruse to the envelope where you spared your G-CODE. Select the correct G-CODE and press enter. In case that everything was associated right, you should see you gadget beginning to plot on the paper.

In case you need to end the procedure, simply press x and the gadget will stop whatever it was doing.

How to Generate Your Own G-Code:

We referenced that Inkscape is the product we will use to create our G-CODES. In this model we will make a basic book (HELLO WORLD) as demonstrated as follows.

Note: Inkscape has no in manufactured method for sparing records as G-CODE. In this manner you need to introduce an Add-on that empowers the fare pictures to G-CODE records. Install this MakerBot Unicorn module from here with establishment notes.

In the event that the establishment was fruitful, Open the Inkscape, go to File menu and snap "Report Properties". First change measurements from px to mm. Additionally lessen the width and stature to 90 mm. Presently close this window. A square shows up as the drawing territory. This is the region that we will use to compose our content.

Presently on the left side bar, click on the make and alter content item tab. Type the content "Hi WORLD" and position it at the upper right corner of the square as demonstrated as follows.

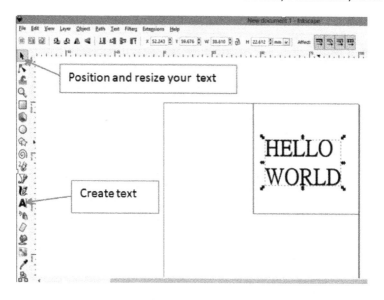

Snap message and pick the sort of textual style that you like. Snap apply and the nearby.

Presently click on way and select **"article to way"**

Your content is presently fit to be spared as G-CODE. Snap on document - > spare as and after that type the record name as "hi world"

Change the document type to "MakerBot Unicon G-Code" as appeared in beneath pic. This will possibly show up if the Add-on establishment was effective. At long last snap on spare and snap alright on the spring up window.

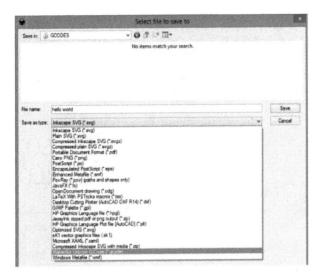

You have produced a G-Code and it tends to be plot-ted utilizing the past methods.

The GRBL Controller:

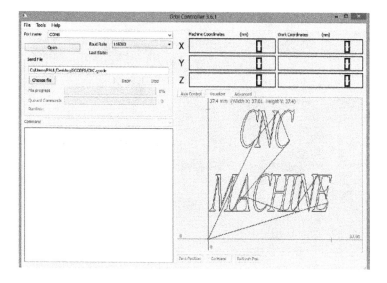

When you've figured out how to produce a G-Code utilizing Inkscape, it might be important to see the G-Code so as to guarantee that it is inside as far as possible.

As far as possible are set in the Arduino CNC CODE in the lines demonstrated as follows:

```
                    CNC_code | Arduino 1.6.6 Hourly Build 2015/06/25 09:34
File  Edit  Sketch  Tools  Help

  CNC_code §

// Motor steps to go 1 millimeter.
// Use test sketch to go 100 steps. Measure the length of line.
// Calculate steps per mm. Enter here.
float StepsPerMillimeterX = 100.0;
float StepsPerMillimeterY = 100.0;

// Drawing robot limits, in mm
// OK to start with. Could go up to 50 mm if calibrated well.
float Xmin = 0;
float Xmax = 40;   //changed this from 40 to 60 cause i used printer drive mechan
float Ymin = 0;
float Ymax = 40;
float Zmin = 0;
float Zmax = 1;

float Xpos = Xmin;
float Ypos = Ymin;
float Zpos = Zmax;

// Set to true to get debug output.
boolean verbose = false;
```

The picture as show above in the GRBL controller ought not go past those farthest point as appeared in the CNC Arduino code above. On the off chance that it goes past those farthest point for instance towards the negative side of the x-hub, that part on the negative side won't be plotted.

In this model x and y esteems run from 0mm to 40mm.

Since I am utilizing printer parts which can plot on a bigger zone, I change the maximum qualities from 40mm to 60mm.

At whatever point you produce a G-Code utilizing Inkscape, you would first be able to open that G-Code in the GRBL program to see whether it is inside those breaking points. If not inside, you have to resize you picture in the Inkscape until it is inside your points of confinement.

So this is the modest and most straightforward technique to assemble a CNC Plotter machine utilizing arduino uno at home.

Code

```
/*
 Send GCODE to this Sketch using gctrl.pde https://github.com/damellis/gctrl
 Convert SVG to GCODE with MakerBot Unicorn plugin for Inkscape available here https://github.com/martymcguire/inkscape-unicorn
 Arduino code for this Mini CNC Plotter based on: https://github.com/adidax/mini_cnc_plotter_firmware
*/
#include <Servo.h>
#include <AFMotor.h>
#define LINE_BUFFER_LENGTH 512
char STEP = MICROSTEP ;
// Servo position for Up and Down
const int penZUp = 115;
const int penZDown = 83;
// Servo on PWM pin 10
const int penServoPin = 10 ;
// Should be right for DVD steppers, but is not too im-
```

portant here

```
const int stepsPerRevolution = 48;
// create servo object to control a servo
Servo penServo;
// Initialize steppers for X- and Y-axis using this Arduino pins for the L293D H-bridge
AF_Stepper myStepperY(stepsPerRevolution,1);
AF_Stepper myStepperX(stepsPerRevolution,2);
/* Structures, global variables  */
struct point {
 float x;
 float y;
 float z;
};
// Current position of plothead
struct point actuatorPos;
// Drawing settings, should be OK
float StepInc = 1;
int StepDelay = 0;
int LineDelay =0;
int penDelay = 50;
// Motor steps to go 1 millimeter.
// Use test sketch to go 100 steps. Measure the length of line.
// Calculate steps per mm. Enter here.
float StepsPerMillimeterX = 100.0;
float StepsPerMillimeterY = 100.0;
// Drawing robot limits, in mm
// OK to start with. Could go up to 50 mm if calibrated
```

well.

```
float Xmin = 0;
float Xmax = 40;
float Ymin = 0;
float Ymax = 40;
float Zmin = 0;
float Zmax = 1;

float Xpos = Xmin;
float Ypos = Ymin;
float Zpos = Zmax;

// Set to true to get debug output.
boolean verbose = false;

// Needs to interpret
// G1 for moving
// G4 P300 (wait 150ms)
// M300 S30 (pen down)
// M300 S50 (pen up)
// Discard anything with a (
// Discard any other command!
/***********************
 * void setup() - Initialisations
***********************/
void setup() {
  // Setup


  Serial.begin( 9600 );


  penServo.attach(penServoPin);
```

```
penServo.write(penZUp);
delay(100);
// Decrease if necessary
myStepperX.setSpeed(600);
myStepperY.setSpeed(600);


  // Set & move to initial default position
// TBD
// Notifications!!!
Serial.println("Mini CNC Plotter alive and kicking!");
Serial.print("X range is from ");
Serial.print(Xmin);
Serial.print(" to ");
Serial.print(Xmax);
Serial.println(" mm.");
Serial.print("Y range is from ");
Serial.print(Ymin);
Serial.print(" to ");
Serial.print(Ymax);
Serial.println(" mm.");
}
/***********************
* void loop() - Main loop
*********************** /
void loop()
{

  delay(100);
```

```
char line[ LINE_BUFFER_LENGTH ];
char c;
int lineIndex;
bool lineIsComment, lineSemiColon;

lineIndex = 0;
lineSemiColon = false;
lineIsComment = false;
while (1) {
  // Serial reception - Mostly from Grbl, added semi-
colon support
  while ( Serial.available()>0 ) {
   c = Serial.read();
   if(( c == '\n') || (c == '\r')) {      // End of line reached
    if( lineIndex > 0 ) {           // Line is complete. Then
execute!
      line[ lineIndex ] = '\0';         // Terminate string
      if(verbose) {
       Serial.print( "Received : ");
       Serial.println( line );
      }
      processIncomingLine( line, lineIndex );
      lineIndex = 0;
    }
    else {
     // Empty or comment line. Skip block.
    }
    lineIsComment = false;
    lineSemiColon = false;
    Serial.println("ok");
   }
```

```
  else {
   if((lineIsComment)||(lineSemiColon)){  // Throw
away all comment characters
     if ( c == ')' )  lineIsComment = false;    // End of
comment. Resume line.
   }
   else {
    if( c <= '' ){                // Throw away whitepace and
control characters
    }
     else if ( c == '/' ) {             // Block delete not
supported. Ignore character.
    }
     else if( c == '(' ) {          // Enable comments flag
and ignore all characters until ')' or EOL.
    lineIsComment = true;
    }
   else if( c == ';' ) {
    lineSemiColon = true;
    }
   else if( lineIndex >= LINE_BUFFER_LENGTH-1 ){
    Serial.println( "ERROR - lineBuffer overflow" );
    lineIsComment = false;
    lineSemiColon = false;
    }
   else if( c >= 'a' && c <= 'z' ){    // Upcase lowercase
    line[ lineIndex++ ] = c-'a'+'A';
    }
   else {
    line[ lineIndex++ ] = c;
```

```
        }
      }
     }
    }
   }
  }
void processIncomingLine( char* line, int charNB ) {
 int currentIndex = 0;
 char buffer[ 64 ];              // Hope that 64 is enough
for 1 parameter
 struct point newPos;
 newPos.x = 0.0;
 newPos.y = 0.0;
 // Needs to interpret
 // G1 for moving
 // G4 P300 (wait 150ms)
 // G1 X60 Y30
 // G1 X30 Y50
 // M300 S30 (pen down)
 // M300 S50 (pen up)
 // Discard anything with a (
 // Discard any other command!
 while( currentIndex < charNB ) {
   switch ( line[ currentIndex++ ] ) {        // Select
command, if any
  case 'U':
   penUp();
   break;
  case 'D':
   penDown();
```

```
  break;
 case 'G':
  buffer[0] = line[ currentIndex++ ];        // /!\ Dirty -
Only works with 2 digit commands
  //   buffer[1] = line[ currentIndex++ ];
  //   buffer[2] = '\0';
  buffer[1] = '\0';

  switch ( atoi( buffer )){        // Select G command
  case 0:                  // G00 & G01 - Movement or fast
movement. Same here
  case 1:
   // /!\ Dirty - Suppose that X is before Y
    char* indexX = strchr( line+currentIndex, 'X' ); //
Get X/Y position in the string (if any)
   char* indexY = strchr( line+currentIndex, 'Y' );
   if ( indexY <= 0 ) {
    newPos.x = atof( indexX + 1);
    newPos.y = actuatorPos.y;
   }
   else if ( indexX <= 0 ) {
    newPos.y = atof( indexY + 1);
    newPos.x = actuatorPos.x;
   }
   else {
    newPos.y = atof( indexY + 1);
    indexY = '\0';
    newPos.x = atof( indexX + 1);
   }
   drawLine(newPos.x, newPos.y );
   //    Serial.println("ok");
```

```
  actuatorPos.x = newPos.x;
  actuatorPos.y = newPos.y;
  break;
 }
 break;
case 'M':
   buffer[0] = line[ currentIndex++ ];        // /!\ Dirty -
Only works with 3 digit commands
  buffer[1] = line[ currentIndex++ ];
  buffer[2] = line[ currentIndex++ ];
  buffer[3] = '\0';
  switch ( atoi( buffer ) ){
  case 300:
   {
    char* indexS = strchr( line+currentIndex, 'S' );
    float Spos = atof( indexS + 1);
    //    Serial.println("ok");
    if(Spos == 30){
     penDown();
    }
    if(Spos == 50){
     penUp();
    }
    break;
   }
  case 114:              // M114 - Repport position
   Serial.print( "Absolute position : X = " );
   Serial.print( actuatorPos.x );
   Serial.print( " - Y = " );
   Serial.println( actuatorPos.y );
```

```
   break;
  default:
   Serial.print( "Command not recognized : M");
   Serial.println( buffer );
  }
 }
 }
}
/*********************************
* Draw a line from (x0;y0) to (x1;y1).
* int (x1;y1) : Starting coordinates
* int (x2;y2) : Ending coordinates
********************************* /
void drawLine(float x1, float y1) {
 if (verbose)
 {
  Serial.print("fx1, fy1: ");
  Serial.print(x1);
  Serial.print(",");
  Serial.print(y1);
  Serial.println("");
 }
 // Bring instructions within limits
 if (x1 >= Xmax) {
  x1 = Xmax;
 }
 if (x1 <= Xmin) {
  x1 = Xmin;
 }
 if (y1 >= Ymax) {
```

```
 y1 = Ymax;
}
if (y1 <= Ymin) {
 y1 = Ymin;
}
if (verbose)
{
 Serial.print("Xpos, Ypos: ");
 Serial.print(Xpos);
 Serial.print(",");
 Serial.print(Ypos);
 Serial.println("");
}
if (verbose)
{
 Serial.print("x1, y1: ");
 Serial.print(x1);
 Serial.print(",");
 Serial.print(y1);
 Serial.println("");
}
// Convert coordinates to steps
x1 = (int)(x1*StepsPerMillimeterX);
y1 = (int)(y1*StepsPerMillimeterY);
float x0 = Xpos;
float y0 = Ypos;
// Let's find out the change for the coordinates
long dx = abs(x1-x0);
long dy = abs(y1-y0);
int sx = x0<x1 ? StepInc : -StepInc;
```

```
int sy = y0<y1 ? StepInc : -StepInc;
long i;
long over = 0;
if (dx > dy) {
 for (i=0; i<dx; ++i) {
  myStepperX.onestep(sx,STEP);
  over+=dy;
  if(over>=dx) {
   over-=dx;
   myStepperY.onestep(sy,STEP);
  }
  delay(StepDelay);
 }
}
else {
 for (i=0; i<dy; ++i) {
  myStepperY.onestep(sy,STEP);
  over+=dx;
  if(over>=dy) {
   over-=dy;
   myStepperX.onestep(sx,STEP);
  }
  delay(StepDelay);
 }
}
if(verbose)
{
 Serial.print("dx, dy:");
 Serial.print(dx);
 Serial.print(",");
```

```
 Serial.print(dy);
 Serial.println("");
}
if(verbose)
{
 Serial.print("Going to (");
 Serial.print(x0);
 Serial.print(",");
 Serial.print(y0);
 Serial.println(")");
}
// Delay before any next lines are submitted
delay(LineDelay);
// Update the positions
Xpos = x1;
Ypos = y1;
}
// Raises pen
void penUp() {
 penServo.write(penZUp);
 delay(penDelay);
 Zpos=Zmax;
 digitalWrite(15, LOW);
  digitalWrite(16, HIGH);
 if(verbose) {
  Serial.println("Pen up!");


 }
}
```

```
// Lowers pen
void penDown() {
 penServo.write(penZDown);
 delay(penDelay);
 Zpos=Zmin;
 digitalWrite(15, HIGH);
  digitalWrite(16, LOW);
 if(verbose) {
  Serial.println("Pen down.");
 }
}
```

ARDUINO
TOUCH SCREEN
CALCULATOR
UTILIZING TFT LCD

Arduino has consistently assembled activities effectively and make them look increasingly alluring. Programming a LCD screen with contact screen alternative may sound as a muddled errand, yet the Arduino libraries and shields had made it extremely simple. In this task we will utilize a 2.4" Arduino TFT LCD screen to fabricate our very own Arduino Touch Screen mini-computer that could play out every single fundamental figuring like Addition, Subtraction, Division and Multiplication.

Materials Required:

- Arduino Uno

- 9V Battery

- 2.4" TFT LCD show Shield.

Getting to know the TFT LCD Screen Module:

Before we really plunge into the task it is essential to know, how this 2.4" TFT LCD Module works and what are the sorts present in it. Give us a chance to investigate the pinouts of this 2.4" TFT LCD screen module.

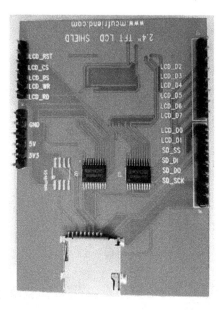

As should be obvious there are 28 pins which will superbly fit into any Arduino Uno/Arduino Mega Board. A little grouping of these pins is given in the table beneath.

Pin Name	Category
LCD_RST	LCD Command Pins
LCD_CS	
LCD_RS	
LCS_WR	
LCD_RD	
LCD_D0	LCD Data Pins
LCD_D1	
LCD_D2	
LCD_D3	
LCD_D4	
LCD_D5	
LCD_D6	
LCD_D7	
SD_SS	SD Card Data Pins
SD_DI	
SD_DO	
SD_SCK	
GND	Power Pins
5V	
3.3V	

As should be obvious the pins can be grouped in to four fundamental groupings, for example, LCD Command Pins, LCD Data Pins, SD Card Pins and Power Pins, We need not think a lot about the itemized working of these pins since they will be take care by our Arduino Library.

You can likewise discover a SD card opening at the base of the module appeared above, which can be used to stack a SD card with bmp picture records, and these pictures can be shown in our TFT LCD screen utilizing the Arduino Program.

Another significant thing to note is your Interface IC. There are numerous kinds of TFT modules accessible in the market beginning from the first Adafruit TFT LCD module to modest Chinese clones. A program which works splendidly for your Adafruit shield probably won't work the equivalent for Chinese breakout sheets. Along these lines, it is essential to realize which kinds of LCD show your are holding close by. This detail must be gotten from the merchant. On the off chance that you are having a modest clone like mine, at that point it is most presumably utilizing the ili9341 driver IC. You can pursue this TFT LCD interfacing with Arduino instructional exercise to evaluate some fundamental model projects and get settled with the LCD screen. Additionally look at our other TFT LCD ventures with Arduino here:

- Step by step instructions to Use NeoPixel LED Strip with Arduino and TFT LCD

- Advanced mobile phone Controlled Digital Code Lock utilizing Arduino

Calibrating the TFT LCD Screen for Touch Screen:

On the off chance that you intending to utilize the touch screen capacity of your TFT LCD module, at that point you need to align it to do it work appropriately. A LCD screen without adjustment may work far-fetched, for example you may contact at one spot and the TFT may react for a touch at some other spot. These alignments results won't be comparable for all sheets and henceforth you are left without anyone else to do this.

The most ideal approach to align is to utilize the adjustment model program (accompanies library) or utilize the sequential screen to recognize your blunder. Anyway for this task since the size of catches is huge adjustment ought not be a major issue and I will likewise clarify how you can align your screen under the programming area underneath.

TFT LCD Connections with Arduino:

The 2.4" TFT LCD screen is an ideal Arduino Shield. You can straightforwardly push the LCD screen over the Arduino Uno and it will flawlessly coordinate with the pins and slid in through. Notwithstanding, as issues of security spread the Programming terminal of your Arduino UNO with a little protection tape, in the event of some unforeseen issue if the terminal interacts with your TFT LCD screen. The LCD collected on UNO will look like underneath.

Programming your Arduino for TFT LCD:

We are utilizing the SPFD5408 Library to get this arduino number cruncher code working. This is an altered library of Adafruit and can work consistently with our LCD TFT Module. You can check the total program toward the finish of this Article.

Note: It is significant for you to introduce this library in your Arduino IDE or this program to aggregate with no blunder.

To introduce this library, you can basically tap on the connection above which will take you to a Github page. There click on clone or download and select "Download ZIP". A compress record will be downloaded.

Presently, open Arduino IDE as well as select Sketch - > Include Librarey - > Add .ZIP library. A program window will open explore to the ZIP record and snap "alright". You should see "Library added to your Libraries" on the base left corner of Arduino, if fruitful. A stepwise manual for do the equivalent is given in the Interfacing Tutorial.

Presently, you can utilize the code beneath in your Arduino IDE and transfer it to your Arduino UNO for the Touch Screen Calculator to work. Further down, I have clarified the code into little portions.

We require 3 libraries for this program to work; all these 3 libraries are given in the ZIP record you installed from the above gave interface. I have essentially included them in the code as demonstrated as follows.

```
#include <SPFD5408_Adafruit_GFX.h>     // Core
graphics library

#include    <SPFD5408_Adafruit_TFTLCD.h>    //
Hardware-specific library

#include <SPFD5408_TouchScreen.h>
```

As said before we have to adjust the LCD screen to make it function true to form, however don't stress the qualities given here are practically general. The factors TS_MINX, TS_MINY, TS_MAXX, and TS_MAXY choose the alignment of the Screen. You can toy around them in the event that you feel the adjustment isn't good.

```
#define TS_MINX 125

#define TS_MINY 85

#define TS_MAXX 965

#define TS_MAXY 905
```

As we probably am aware the TFT LCD screen can show a ton of hues, every one of these hues must be entered in hex worth. To make it increasingly comprehensible we allot these qualities to a variable as demonstrated as follows.

Note: The qualities are genuine just if the screen is turn by 2. This is for programming comfort.

```
#define WHITE  0x0000 //Black->White

#define YELLOW  0x001F //Blue->Yellow

#define CYAN   0xF800 //Red->Cyan

#define PINK  0x07E0 //Green-> Pink

#define RED   0x07FF //Cyan -> Red
```

```
#define GREEN 0xF81F //Pink -> Green

#define BLUE  0xFFE0 //Yellow->Blue

#define BLACK  0xFFFF //White-> Black
```

OK now, we can get into the programming part. There are three areas associated with this program. One is making a UI of a number cruncher with catches and show. At that point, recognizing the catches dependent on the clients contact lastly ascertaining the outcomes and show them. Give us a chance to traverse them individually.

1. Making a UI of Calculator:

This is the place you can utilize a great deal of your innovativeness to plan the User Interface of adding machine. I have basically made a fundamental design of a mini-computer with 16 Buttons and one showcase unit. You need to develop the structure simply like you will draw something on MS paint. The libraries added will enable you to draw Lines, Rectangle, Circles, Chars, Strings and part a greater amount of any favored shading. You can comprehend the accessible capacities from this article.

I have utilized the line and box attracting capacities to plan a UI which looks fundamentally the same as the 90's adding machine. Each container has a width and tallness of 60 pixels.

//Draw the Result Box

tft.fillRect(0, 0, 240, 80, CYAN);

//Draw First Column

tft.fillRect (0,260,60,60,RED);

tft.fillRect (0,200,60,60,BLACK);

tft.fillRect (0,140,60,60,BLACK);

tft.fillRect (0,80,60,60,BLACK);

```
//Draw Third Column

  tft.fillRect (120,260,60,60,GREEN);

  tft.fillRect (120,200,60,60,BLACK);

  tft.fillRect (120,140,60,60,BLACK);

  tft.fillRect (120,80,60,60,BLACK);

  //Draw Secound & Fourth Column

  for (int b=260; b>=80; b-=60)

{ tft.fillRect (180,b,60,60,BLUE);

   tft.fillRect (60,b,60,60,BLACK);}

  //Draw Horizontal Lines

  for (int h=80; h<=320; h+=60)

  tft.drawFastHLine(0, h, 240, WHITE);

  //Draw Vertical Lines

  for (int v=0; v<=240; v+=60)

  tft.drawFastVLine(v, 80, 240, WHITE);
```

```
//Display keypad lables

for (int j=0;j<4;j++) {

  for (int i=0;i<4;i++) {

    tft.setCursor(22 + (60*i), 100 + (60*j));

    tft.setTextSize(3);

    tft.setTextColor(WHITE);

    tft.println(symbol[j][i]);
```

2. Distinguishing the catches:

Another difficult undertaking is distinguishing the client contact. Each time the client contacts some place we will ready to how where the X and Y position of the pixel he contacted. This worth can be shown on the sequential screen utilizing the println as demonstrated as follows.

```
TSPoint p = waitTouch();

X = p.y; Y = p.x;

Serial.print(X); Serial.print(','); Serial.println(Y);//
```

```
+ " " + Y);
```

Since we have planned the container with width and tallness of 60 pixel each and have four Rows and for sections beginning from (0,0). The situation of each case can be anticipated as appeared in underneath picture.

However, in commonsense case, this won't be the outcome. There will be a major distinction between the normal and genuine worth, because of the adjustment issue.

In this way, to anticipate the careful situation of the crate, you need to tap on hold and check its relating position on the sequential screen. This probably won't be most expert method for doing it, yet at the mean time it works consummately. I quantified the situation of the considerable number of lines and acquired the beneath values.

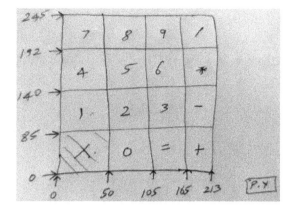

Presently, since we know the situation of all the cases. At the point when a client contacts anyplace we can anticipate where he has moved by contrasting his (X,Y) values with the incentive for each crate as demonstrated as follows.

```
if (X<105 && X>50) //Detecting Buttons on Col-
umn 2

{

  if(Y>0 && Y<85)

  {Serial.println ("Button 0"); //Button 0 is Pressed

  if(Number==0)

  Number=0;
```

```
else

Number = (Number*10) + 0; //Pressed twice

}

if (Y > 85 && Y < 140)

{Serial.println ("Button 2");

if (Number==0)

Number=2;

else

Number = (Number*10) + 2; //Pressed twice

}
```

3. Showing Numbers and Calculating the Result:

The last advance is to ascertain the outcome and show them on TFT LCD Screen. This arduino mini-computer can perform activity with 2 numbers as it were. These two numbers are named as factors "Num1" and "Num2". The variable "Number" gives and takes an incentive from Num1 as well as Num2 as well as furthermore bears the outcome.

At the point when an utilization presses a catch, one

digit is added to number. At the point when another catch is squeezed, the past one digit is increased with 10 and the new number is included with it. For instance, in the event that we press 8 and, at that point press 5 and afterward press 7. At that point first the variable will hold 8 at that point $(8*10)+5=85$ at that point $(85*10)+7 = 857$. So at long last the variable will have the worth 857 with it.

```
if(Y>192 && Y<245)

  {Serial.println ("Button 8");

   if(Number==0)

   Number=8;

   else

   Number = (Number*10) + 8; //Pressed again

   }
```

At the point when we play out any activity like expansion, when the clients presses the expansion button the incentive from Number will be moved to Num1 and after that Number will be made zero with the goal that it prepares to take the contribution for second number.

At the point when Equal is squeezed the incentive in Number will be sent to Num2 and afterward the separate figuring (for this situation expansion) will be made and the outcome will be again put away in the variable "Number".

At last this worth will be shown in the LCD screen.

Working:

The working of this Arduino Touch Screen Calculator is straightforward. You need to transfer the beneath given code on your Arduino and fire it up. You get the adding machine showed on your LCD screen.

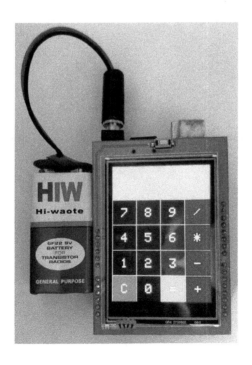

Presently, you can enter any number and play out your counts. It is restricted to just two operand and administrator until further notice. However, you can change the code to cause it to have heaps of alternative.

You need to press the "C" to clear the incentive on screen each time in the wake of playing out a figuring. Expectation you comprehended the venture and appreciated structure something comparable. See you next with another fascinating undertaking up to that point glad registering!!

Code

```
/*_____Import Libraries_____*/
#include <SPFD5408_Adafruit_GFX.h>      // Core
graphics library
#include <SPFD5408_Adafruit_TFTLCD.h> // Hard-
ware-specific library
#include <SPFD5408_TouchScreen.h>
/*_____End of Libraries_____*/
/*_____Define LCD pins (I have asigned the default
values)_____*/
#define YP A1 // must be an analog pin, use "An" nota-
tion!
#define XM A2 // must be an analog pin, use "An" nota-
tion!
#define YM 7 // can be a digital pin
#define XP 6 // can be a digital pin
```

```
#define LCD_CS A3
#define LCD_CD A2
#define LCD_WR A1
#define LCD_RD A0
#define LCD_RESET A4
/*_____End of defanitions_____*/
/*_____Assign names to colors and pressure_____*/
#define WHITE  0x0000 //Black->White
#define YELLOW  0x001F //Blue->Yellow
#define CYAN  0xF800 //Red->Cyan
#define PINK  0x07E0 //Green-> Pink
#define RED  0x07FF //Cyan -> Red
#define GREEN 0xF81F //Pink -> Green
#define BLUE 0xFFE0 //Yellow->Blue
#define BLACK  0xFFFF //White-> Black
#define MINPRESSURE 10
#define MAXPRESSURE 1000
/*_____Assigned_____*/
/*____Calibrate TFT LCD_____*/
#define TS_MINX 125
#define TS_MINY 85
#define TS_MAXX 965
#define TS_MAXY 905
/*_____End of Calibration_____*/
```

TouchScreen ts = TouchScreen(XP, YP, XM, YM, 300); //300 is the sensitivity
Adafruit_TFTLCD tft(LCD_CS, LCD_CD, LCD_WR, LCD_RD, LCD_RESET); //Start communication with LCD

```
String symbol[4][4] = {
 { "7", "8", "9", "/" },
 { "4", "5", "6", "'*'" },
 { "1", "2", "3", "-" },
 { "C", "0", "=", "+" }
};
int X,Y;
long Num1,Num2,Number;
char action;
boolean result = false;
void setup() {
  Serial.begin(9600); //Use serial monitor for debugging
 tft.reset(); //Always reset at start
 tft.begin(0x9341); // My LCD uses LIL9341 Interface driver IC
 tft.setRotation(2); // I just roated so that the power jack faces up - optional
 tft.fillScreen(WHITE);
 IntroScreen();

  draw_BoxNButtons();
}
void loop() {
TSPoint p = waitTouch();
X = p.y; Y = p.x;
//  Serial.print(X); Serial.print(','); Serial.println(Y);//
+ " " + Y);
DetectButtons();
```

```
if(result==true)
CalculateResult();
DisplayResult();
 delay(300);
}
TSPoint waitTouch() {
 TSPoint p;
 do {
  p = ts.getPoint();
  pinMode(XM, OUTPUT);
  pinMode(YP, OUTPUT);
  } while((p.z  < MINPRESSURE )|| (p.z > MAXPRES-
SURE));
 p.x = map(p.x, TS_MINX, TS_MAXX, 0, 320);
 p.y = map(p.y, TS_MINY, TS_MAXY, 0, 240);;
 return p;
}
void DetectButtons()
{


  if(X<50 && X>0) //Detecting Buttons on Column 1
{
  if(Y>0 && Y<85) //If cancel Button is pressed
   {Serial.println ("Button Cancel"); Number=Num1=
Num2=0; result=false;}


    if(Y>85 && Y<140) //If Button 1 is pressed
  {Serial.println ("Button 1");
```

```
if (Number==0)
Number=1;
else
Number = (Number*10) + 1; //Pressed twice
}


  if (Y>140 && Y<192) //If Button 4 is pressed
{Serial.println ("Button 4");
if (Number==0)
Number=4;
else
Number = (Number*10) + 4; //Pressed twice
}


  if (Y>192 && Y<245) //If Button 7 is pressed
{Serial.println ("Button 7");
if (Number==0)
Number=7;
else
Number = (Number*10) + 7; //Pressed twice
}
}
  if (X<105 && X>50) //Detecting Buttons on Column
2
{
if (Y>0 && Y<85)
{Serial.println ("Button 0"); //Button 0 is Pressed
if (Number==0)
Number=0;
```

```
else
Number = (Number*10) + 0; //Pressed twice
}


   if(Y>85 && Y<140)
{Serial.println ("Button 2");
 if(Number==0)
Number=2;
else
Number = (Number*10) + 2; //Pressed twice
}


   if(Y>140 && Y<192)
{Serial.println ("Button 5");
 if(Number==0)
Number=5;
else
Number = (Number*10) + 5; //Pressed twic
}


   if(Y>192 && Y<245)
{Serial.println ("Button 8");
 if(Number==0)
Number=8;
else
Number = (Number*10) + 8; //Pressed twic
}
}
```

```
   if (X<165 && X>105) //Detecting Buttons on Col-
umn 3
 {
  if(Y>0 && Y<85)
  {Serial.println ("Button Equal");
  Num2=Number;
  result = true;
  }


    if(Y>85 && Y<140)
  {Serial.println ("Button 3");
   if(Number==0)
  Number=3;
  else
  Number = (Number*10) + 3; //Pressed twice
  }


    if(Y>140 && Y<192)
  {Serial.println ("Button 6");
  if(Number==0)
  Number=6;
  else
  Number = (Number*10) + 6; //Pressed twice
  }


    if(Y>192 && Y<245)
  {Serial.println ("Button 9");
  if(Number==0)
```

```
 Number=9;
 else
 Number = (Number*10) + 9; //Pressed twice
 }
}

   if (X<213 && X>165) //Detecting Buttons on Col-
umn 3
{
 Num1 = Number;
 Number =0;
 tft.setCursor(200, 20);
 tft.setTextColor(RED);
 if(Y>0 && Y<85)
      {Serial.println ("Addition"); action = 1; tft.
println('+');}
  if(Y>85 && Y<140)
     {Serial.println ("Subtraction"); action = 2; tft.
println('-');}
  if(Y>140 && Y<192)
    {Serial.println ("Multiplication"); action = 3; tft.
println('*');}
  if(Y>192 && Y<245)
      {Serial.println ("Devesion"); action = 4; tft.
println('/');}
  delay(300);
 }
}
void CalculateResult()
{
 if(action==1)
```

```
 Number = Num1+Num2;
if(action==2)
 Number = Num1-Num2;
if(action==3)
 Number = Num1*Num2;
if(action==4)
 Number = Num1/Num2;
}
void DisplayResult()
{
  tft.fillRect(0, 0, 240, 80, CYAN); //clear result box
  tft.setCursor(10, 20);
  tft.setTextSize(4);
  tft.setTextColor(BLACK);
  tft.println(Number); //update new value
}
void IntroScreen()
{
 tft.setCursor (55, 120);
 tft.setTextSize (3);
 tft.setTextColor(RED);
 tft.println("ARDUINO");
 tft.setCursor (30, 160);
 tft.println("CALCULATOR");
 tft.setCursor (30, 220);
 tft.setTextSize (2);
 tft.setTextColor(BLUE);
 tft.println("-Hello world");
 delay(1800);
}
```

```
void draw_BoxNButtons()
{
 //Draw the Result Box
 tft.fillRect(0, 0, 240, 80, CYAN);

 //Draw First Column
 tft.fillRect (0,260,60,60,RED);
 tft.fillRect (0,200,60,60,BLACK);
 tft.fillRect (0,140,60,60,BLACK);
 tft.fillRect (0,80,60,60,BLACK);

 //Draw Third Column
 tft.fillRect (120,260,60,60,GREEN);
 tft.fillRect (120,200,60,60,BLACK);
 tft.fillRect (120,140,60,60,BLACK);
 tft.fillRect (120,80,60,60,BLACK);

 //Draw Secound & Fourth Column
 for (int b=260; b>=80; b-=60)
 { tft.fillRect (180,b,60,60,BLUE);
  tft.fillRect (60,b,60,60,BLACK);}

 //Draw Horizontal Lines
 for (int h=80; h<=320; h+=60)
 tft.drawFastHLine(0, h, 240, WHITE);

 //Draw Vertical Lines
 for (int v=0; v<=240; v+=60)
 tft.drawFastVLine(v, 80, 240, WHITE);

 //Display keypad lables
 for (int j=0;j<4;j++) {
  for (int i=0;i<4;i++) {
   tft.setCursor(22 + (60*i), 100 + (60*j));
   tft.setTextSize(3);
   tft.setTextColor(WHITE);
```

```
    tft.println(symbol[j][i]);
  }
 }
}
```

❖ ❖ ❖

HOW TO CONTROL STEPPER MOTOR UTILIZING POTENTIOMETER AND ARDUINO

Stepper engines are progressively taking its situation in the realm of the gadgets. Beginning from an ordinary Surveillance camera to a muddled CNC machines/ Robot these Stepper Motors are utilized wherever as actuators since they give exact controlling. In this instructional exercise we will find out about the most usually/inexpensively accessible stepper engine 28-BYJ48 and how to interface it with Arduino utilizing ULN2003 stepper module.

In last venture we have basically Interfaced Stepper Motor with Arduino, where you can turn the stepper engine by entering the revolution edge in Serial Monitor of Arduino. Here in this undertaking, we will Rotate the Stepper Motor utilizing Potentiometer and Arduino, as in the event that you turn the potentiometer clockwise, at that point stepper will pivot clockwise and on the off chance that you turn potentiometer anticlockwise, at that point it will turn anticlockwise.

Stepper Motors:

Give us a chance to investigate this 28-BYJ48 Stepper engine.

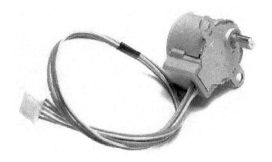

Alright, so not at all like a typical DC engine this one has five wires of every single extravagant shading leaving it and for what reason is it so? To comprehend this we should initially realize how a stepper functions and what its strength is. As a matter of first importance steppers engines don't pivot, they step thus they otherwise called venture engines. Which means, they will move just slowly and carefully. These engines have an arrangement of loops present in them and these curls must be empowered in a specific manner to cause the engine to turn. At the point when each loop is being stimulated the engine makes a stride and a succession of empowerment will make the engine make consistent strides, subsequently making it to turn. Give us a chance to investigate the loops present inside the engine to know precisely know from where these wires originate from.

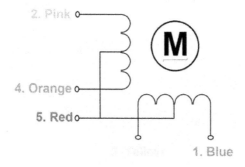

As should be obvious the engine has Unipolar 5-lead loop course of action. There are four curls which must be empowered in a specific arrangement. The Red wires will be provided with +5V and the staying four wires will be dismantled to ground for setting off the individual loop. We utilize a microcontroller like Arduino stimulate these curls in a specific grouping and cause the engine to play out the necessary number of steps.

So now, for what reason is this engine called the 28-BYJ48? Truly!!! I don't have the foggiest idea. There is no specialized explanation behind this engine for being named so; perhaps we should plunge a lot further into it. Give us a chance to take a gander at a portion of the significant specialized information got from the datasheet of this engine in the image beneath.

Rated voltage :	5VDC
Number of Phase	4
Speed Variation Ratio	1/64
Stride Angle	5.625°/64
Frequency	100Hz
DC resistance	50Ω±7%(25°C)
Idle In-traction Frequency	> 600Hz
Idle Out-traction Frequency	> 1000Hz
In-traction Torque	>34.3mN.m(120Hz)
Self-positioning Torque	>34.3mN.m
Friction torque	600-1200 gf.cm
Pull in torque	300 gf.cm
Insulated resistance	>10MΩ(500V)
Insulated electricity power	600VAC/1mA/1s
Insulation grade	A
Rise in Temperature	<40K(120Hz)
Noise	<35dB(120Hz,No load,10cm)
Model	28BYJ-48 – 5V

That is a head brimming with data, however we have to take a gander at couple of significant ones to recognize what sort of stepper we are utilizing so we can program it productively. First we realize that it is a 5V Stepper engine since we stimulate the Red wire with 5V. At that point, we additionally realize that it is a four stage stepper engine since it had four curls in it. Presently, the rigging proportion is given to be 1:64. This implies the pole that you see outside will make one complete revolution just if the engine inside turns for multiple times. This is a direct result of the apparatuses that are associated between the engine and yield shaft, these riggings help in expanding the torque.

Another significant information to notice is the

Stride Angle: 5.625°/64. This implies the engine when works in 8-advance grouping will move 5.625 degree for each progression and it will make 64 strides (5.625*64=360) to finish one full turn.

Calculating the Steps per Revolution for Stepper Motor:

It is imperative to realize how to ascertain the means per Revolution for your stepper engine in light of the fact that at exactly that point you can program it viably.

In Arduino we will work the engine in 4-advance arrangement so the walk edge will be 11.25° since it is 5.625°(given in datasheet) for 8 stage succession it will be 11.25° (5.625*2=11.25).

Steps per upset = 360/advance point

Here, 360/11.25 = 32 stages for each insurgency.

Why so we need Driver modules for Stepper motors?

Most stepper engines will work just with the assistance of a driver module. This is on the grounds that the controller module (For our situation Arduino) won't have the option to give enough current from its I/O pins for the engine to work. So we will utilize an outer module like ULN2003 module as stepper engine driver. There are a numerous kinds of driver module and the rating of one will change dependent on the sort of engine utilized. The essential rule for all driver modules will be to source/sink enough ebb and flow for the engine to work.

Circuit Diagram for Rotating Stepper Motor using Potentiometer:

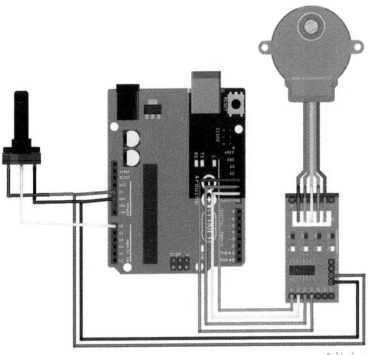

fritzing

The circuit Diagram for the Controlling Stepper Motor utilizing Potentiometer and Arduino is appeared previously. We have utilized the 28BYJ-48 Stepper engine and the ULN2003 Driver module. To invigorate the four curls of the stepper engine we are utilizing the computerized pins 8,9,10 and 11. The driver module is fueled by the 5V stick of the Arduino Board. A potentiometer is associated with A0 situated in whose qualities we will pivot the Stepper engine.

In any case, control the driver with External Power supply when you are associating some heap to the steppe engine. Since I am simply utilizing the engine for exhibit reason I have utilized the +5V rail of the Arduino Board. Likewise make sure to interface the Ground of the Arduino with the ground of the Driver module.

Code for Arduino Board:

Before we start programming with our Arduino, let us comprehend what ought to really occur inside the program. As said before we will utilize 4-advance succession technique so we will have four stages to perform for making one complete revolution.

Step	Pin Energized	Coils Energized
Step 1	8 and 9	A and B
Step 2	9 and 10	B and C
Step 3	10 and 11	C and D
Step 4	11 and 8	D and A

The Driver module will have four LED utilizing which we can check which loop is being empowered at some random time.

In this exercise we are gonna to program the Arduino so that we can turn the potentiometer associated with stick A0 and control the course of the Stepper engine. The total program can be found underneath.

The quantity of steps per transformation for our stepper engine was determined to be 32; thus we enter that as appeared in the line underneath

```
#define STEPS 32
```

Next you need to make examples in which we determine the pins to which we have associated the Stepper engine.

```
Stepper stepper (STEPS, 8, 10, 9, 11);
```

Note: The pins number are scattered as 8,10,9,11 intentionally. You need to pursue a similar example regardless of whether you change the pins to which your engine is associated.

Since we are utilizing the Arduino stepper library, we can set the speed of the engine utilizing the beneath line. The speed can run between 0 to 200 for 28-BYJ48 stepper engines.

```
stepper.setSpeed(200);
```

Presently, to make the engine move one stage clockwise we can utilize the accompanying line.

```
stepper.step(1);
```

To make the engine move one stage hostile to clockwise we can utilize the accompanying line.

```
stepper.step(-1);
```

In our program we will peruse the estimation of the Analog stick A0 and contrast it and past worth (Pval). In case that it has expanded we move 5 stages in clockwise and in case it is diminished, at that point we move 5 stages in against clockwise.

```
potVal = map(analogRead(A0),0,1024,0,500);

if(potVal>Pval)

 stepper.step(5);
```

```
if(potVal<Pval)

stepper.step(-5);

Pval = potVal;
```

Working:

When the association is made the equipment should look like this in the image underneath.

Presently, transfer the underneath program in your Arduino UNO and open the sequential screen. As talked about before you need to turn the potentiometer to control the pivot of the Stepper engine. Pivoting it in clockwise will turn the stepper engine clockwise way and the other way around.

Expectation you comprehended the undertaking and

appreciated structure it.

Code

```
#include <Stepper.h> // Include the header file
// change this to the number of steps on your motor
#define STEPS 32
// create an instance of the stepper class using the
steps and pins
Stepper stepper(STEPS, 8, 10, 9, 11);
int Pval = 0;
int potVal = 0;
void setup() {
 Serial.begin(9600);
 stepper.setSpeed(200);
}
void loop() {
potVal = map(analogRead(A0),0,1024,0,500);
if(potVal>Pval)
 stepper.step(5);
if(potVal<Pval)
 stepper.step(-5);
Pval = potVal;
Serial.println(Pval); //for debugging
}
```

◆ ◆ ◆

AC VOLTMETER UTILIZING ARDUINO

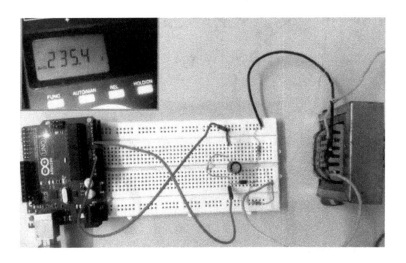

In this undertaking, AC Voltage Measuring Device utilizing Arduino will gauge the voltage of Alternating Current Supply at our home. We are gonna to print that voltage on sequential screen of Arduino IDE just as show on the multimeter.

Making a Digital Voltmeter is a great deal simple than making a simple one in light of the fact that if there should arise an occurrence of simple voltmeter you should have great information of physical parameters like torque, grating misfortunes and so on though in the event of computerized voltmeter you can simply utilize a LCD or LED grid or even your workstation (as for this situation) to print the voltage esteems for you. Here are some Digital Voltmeter Projects:

- Basic Digital Voltmeter Circuit with PCB utilizing ICL7107

- LM3914 Voltmeter Circuit

- 0-25V Digital Voltmeter utilizing AVR Micro-controller

Required Components:

- 1N4007 diode
- One 12-0-12 transformer
- Resistors 10k; 4.7k.
- 1uf capacitor
- Zener diode(5v)
- Connecting wires
- Arduino UNO

Arduino Voltmeter Circuit Diagram:

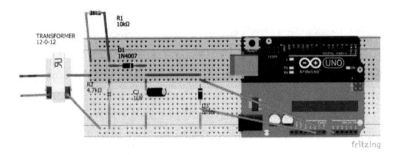

Circuit Diagram for this Arduino Voltmeter is appeared previously.

Associations:

- Associate high voltage side(220V) of transformer to the mains supply and low voltage(12v) to the voltage divider circuit.

- Interface 10k resistor in arrangement with 4.7k resistor yet make a point to accept voltage as contribution crosswise over 4.7k resistor.

- Associate diode as appeared.

- Associate capacitor and zener diode crosswise over 4.7k

- Associate a wire from n-terminal of diode to the simple stick A0 of Arduino.

** Note: Do associate ground stick of Arduino to the point as appeared in the figure or circuit won't work.

Need of voltage divider circuit?

As we are utilizing 220/12 v transformer, we get 12 v on l.v side. Since this voltage isn't reasonable as contribution for Arduino we need a voltage divider circuit which can give appropriate voltage esteem as contribution to Arduino.

Why diode and capacitor is associated?

Since Arduino don't take negative voltage esteems as info, we first need to evacuate negative cycle of venture down AC with the goal that lone positive voltage worth is taken by Arduino. Thus diode is associated with amend the progression down voltage. Check our Half wave rectifier and Full wave Rectifier circuit to get familiar with amendment.

This redressed voltage isn't smooth as it contains enormous waves which can't give us any definite simple worth. Subsequently capacitor is associated with smooth out the a.c signal.

Reason for zener diode?

Arduino can get harm if voltage more prominent than 5v is encouraged to it. Consequently a 5v zener diode is associated with guarantee security of Arduino which breakdowns on the off chance that this voltage surpassed 5v.

Working of Arduino based AC Voltmeter:

1. Venture down voltage is gotten on l.v side of transformer which is reasonable to use crosswise over typical power rating resistors.

2. At that point we get appropriate voltage esteem crosswise over 4.7k resistor

Greatest voltage that can be estimated is found by mimicking this circuit on proteus (clarified in reenactment area).

3. Arduino accepts this voltage as contribution from stick A0 in type of simple qualities between 0 to 1023. 0 being 0 volt and 1023 being 5v.

4. Arduino then changes over this simple incentive into relating mains a.c. voltage by a recipe. (Clarified in code segment).

Simulation:

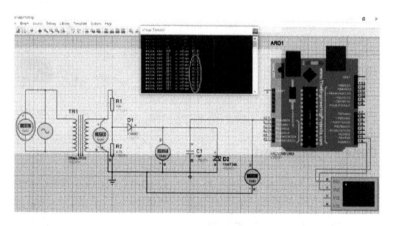

Careful circuit is made in proteus and after that reproduced. To discover greatest voltage that this circuit can gauge hit and preliminary strategy is utilized.

On making alternator's pinnacle voltage 440 (311

r.m.s), voltage on stick A0 was seen as 5 volts for example greatest. Consequently this circuit can quantify greatest 311 r.m.s voltage.

Reenactment is performed for different voltages between 220 r.m.s to 440v.

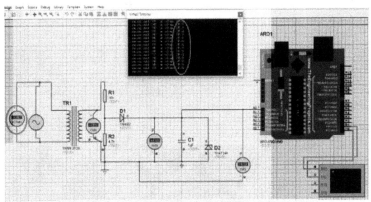

Simulating AC 285 RMS voltage using
AC Arduino Voltmeter

Code Explanation:

Complete ArduinoVoltmeter Code is given toward the finish of this undertaking and it is all around clarified through the remarks. Here we are clarifying couple of part of it.

m is the info simple worth gotten on stick A0 i.e.,

```
m= pinMode (A0,INPUT); // set pin a0 as input pin
```

To allocate variable n to this recipe n=(m*.304177), first some kind of estimations is performed by utilizing the information got in reenactment segment:

As found in reproduction photo, 5v or 1023 simple worth is acquired at stick A0 when information a.c voltage is 311 volts. Consequently:

1023 simple worth relates to 311 volt mains supply

So any arbitrary simple worth relates to (311/1023)*m where m is acquired simple worth.

Thus we land at this equation:

n=(311/1023)*m volts or n=(m*.304177)

Presently this voltage worth is imprinted on the sequential screen by utilizing sequential directions as clarified underneath.

Qualities imprinted on the screen are:
Simple info esteem as determined in the code:

```
Serial.print(" analog input ") ; // this gives name
which is "analog input" to the printed analog value

Serial.print(m);// this simply prints the input ana-
log value
```

Required a.c voltage as indicated in the code:

> Serial.print(" ac voltage "); // this gives name "ac voltage" to the printed analog value
>
> Serial.print(n); // this simply prints the ac voltage value

Code

```
int m;// initialise variable m
float n;//initialise variable n
void setup()
{
 pinMode(A0,INPUT); // set pin a0 as input pin
  Serial.begin(9600);// begin serial communication between arduino and pc
}
void loop()
{
 m=analogRead(A0);// read analog values from pin A0 across capacitor
   n=(m* .304177);// converts analog value(x) into input ac supply value using this formula ( explained in woeking section)


   Serial.print(" analaog input "); // specify name to the corresponding value to be printed
   Serial.print(m); // print input analog value on serial monitor
```

```
  Serial.print(" ac voltage ") ; // specify name to the
corresponding value to be printed
  Serial.print(n) ; // prints the ac value on Serial moni-
tor
  Serial.println();
}
```

❖ ❖ ❖

INTERFACING STEPPER MOTOR WITH ARDUINO UNO

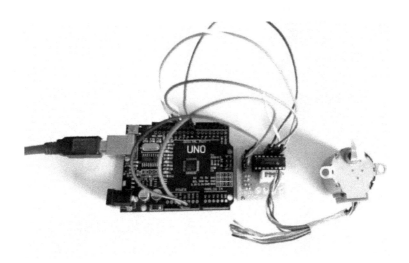

Stepper engines are progressively taking its situation in the realm of the hardware. Beginning from a typical Surveillance camera to a confounded CNC machines/Robot these Stepper Motors are utilized wherever as actuators since they give exact controlling. In this instructional exercise we will find the most regularly/efficiently accessible stepper engine 28-BYJ48 and how to interface it with Arduino utilizing ULN2003 stepper module.

Stepper Motors:

Give us a chance to investigate this 28-BYJ48 Stepper engine.

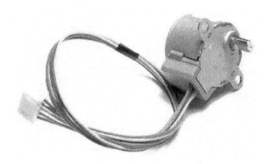

Alright, so not like an ordinary DC engine this one has five wires of every extravagant shading leaving it and for what reason is it so? To comprehend this we should initially realize how a stepper functions and what its claim to fame is. Above all else steppers engines don't pivot, they step thus they otherwise called venture engines. Which means, they will move just slowly and carefully. These engines have a grouping of curls present in them and these loops must be invigorated in a specific manner to cause the engine to pivot. At the point when each curl is being stimulated the engine makes a stride and a succession of empowerment will make the engine make non-stop strides, in this way making it to pivot. Give us a chance to investigate the loops present inside the engine to know precisely know from where these wires originate from.

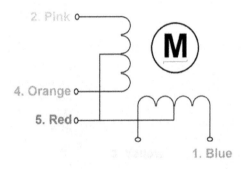

As should be obvious the engine has Unipolar 5-lead curl game plan. There are four loops which must be stimulated in a specific succession. The Red wires will be provided with +5V and the staying four wires will be dismantled to ground for setting off the particular curl. We utilize a microcontroller like Arduino empower these curls in a specific succession and cause the engine to play out the necessary number of steps.

So now, for what reason is this engine called the 28-BYJ48? Truly!!! I don't have the foggiest idea. There is no specialized purpose behind this engine for being named so; perhaps we should jump a lot further into it. Give us a chance to take a gander at a portion of the significant specialized information acquired from the datasheet of this engine in the image underneath.

Rated voltage :	5VDC
Number of Phase	4
Speed Variation Ratio	1/64
Stride Angle	5.625°/64
Frequency	100Hz
DC resistance	50Ω±7%(25℃)
Idle In-traction Frequency	> 600Hz
Idle Out-traction Frequency	> 1000Hz
In-traction Torque	>34.3mN.m(120Hz)
Self-positioning Torque	>34.3mN.m
Friction torque	600-1200 gf.cm
Pull in torque	300 gf.cm
Insulated resistance	>10MΩ(500V)
Insulated electricity power	600VAC/1mA/1s
Insulation grade	A
Rise in Temperature	<40K(120Hz)
Noise	<35dB(120Hz,No load,10cm)
Model	28BYJ-48 – 5V

Technical Data from the Datasheet of Stepper Motor

That is a head loaded with data, yet we have to take a gander at couple of significant ones to recognize what sort of stepper we are utilizing so we can program it productively. First we realize that it is a 5V Stepper engine since we empower the Red wire with 5V. At that point, we likewise realize that it is a four stage stepper engine since it had four curls in it. Presently, the rigging proportion is given to be 1:64. This implies the pole that you see outside will make one complete turn just if the engine inside pivots for multiple times. This is a result of the apparatuses that are associated between the engine and yield shaft, these riggings help in expanding the torque.

Another significant information to notice is the Stride Angle: 5.625°/64. This implies the engine when works in 8-advance succession will move 5.625 degree for each progression and it will make 64 strides (5.625*64=360) to finish one full revolution.

Calculating the Steps per Revolution for Stepper Motor:

It is critical to realize how to ascertain the means per Revolution for your stepper engine in light of the fact that at exactly that point you can program it successfully.

In Arduino we will work the engine in 4-advance succession so the walk point will be 11.25° since it is 5.625°(given in datasheet) for 8 stage grouping it will be 11.25° (5.625*2=11.25).

Steps per transformation = 360/advance edge

Here, 360/11.25 = 32 stages for every upset.

Why so we need Driver modules for Stepper motors?

Most stepper engines will work just with the assistance of a driver module. This is on the grounds that the controller module (For our situation Arduino) won't have the option to give enough current from its I/O pins for the engine to work. So we will utilize an outside module like ULN2003 module as stepper engine driver. There are a numerous sorts of driver module and the rating of one will change dependent on the kind of engine utilized. The essential rule for all driver modules will be to source/sink enough ebb and flow for the engine to work.

Arduino Stepper Motor Control Circuit Diagram and Explanation:

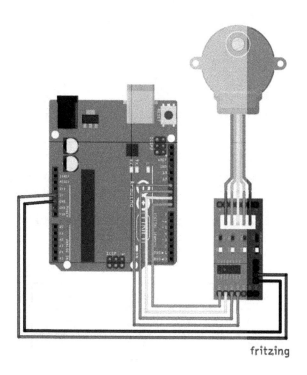

fritzing

The circuit Diagram for the arduino stepper engine control venture is appeared previously. We have utilized the 28BYJ-48 Stepper engine and the ULN2003 Driver module. To empower the four curls of the stepper engine we are utilizing the computerized pins 8,9,10 and 11. The driver module is controlled by the 5V stick of the Arduino Board.

In any case, control the driver with External Power supply when you are associating some heap to the steppe engine. Since I am simply utilizing the engine for exhibit reason I have utilized the +5V rail of the Arduino Board. Likewise make sure to interface the Ground of the Arduino with the ground of the Diver module.

Code for Arduino Board:

Before we start programming with our Arduino, let us comprehend what ought to really occur inside the program. As said before we will utilize 4-advance arrangement strategy so we will have four stages to perform for making one complete turn.

Step	Pin Energized	Coils Energized
Step 1	8 and 9	A and B
Step 2	9 and 10	B and C
Step 3	10 and 11	C and D

Step 4	11 and 8	D and A

The Driver module will have four LED utilizing which we can check which curl is being empowered at some random time.

In this instructional exercise we will compose the arduino stepper engine code and for that we will program the Arduino so that we can enter the quantity of steps to be taken by the stepper engine through the sequential screen of the Arduino. The total program can be found at the finish of the instructional exercise couple of significant lines are clarified beneath.

The quantity of steps per upheaval for our stepper engine was determined to be 32; subsequently we enter that as appeared in the line underneath

```
#define STEPS 32
```

Next you need to make occasions in which we indicate the pins to which we have associated the Stepper engine.

```
Stepper stepper (STEPS, 8, 10, 9, 11);
```

Note: The pins number are scattered as 8,10,9,11 deliberately. You need to pursue a similar example regardless of whether you change the pins to which your engine is associated.

Since we are utilizing the Arduino stepper library, we can set the speed of the engine utilizing the beneath line. The speed can go between 0 to 200 for 28-BYJ48 stepper engines.

```
stepper.setSpeed(200);
```

Presently, to make the engine move one stage we can utilize the accompanying line.

```
stepper.step(val);
```

The quantity of steps to be moved will be given by the variable "val". Since we have 32 stages and 64 as the apparatus proportion we have to move 2048 (32*64=2048), to make one complete pivot.

The estimation of the variable "val" can be entered by the client utilizing the sequential screen.

Working of Stepper Motor with Arduino:

When the association is made the equipment should look something like this in the image beneath.

Presently, transfer the beneath program in your Arduino UNO and open the sequential screen. As talked about before we should make 2048 stages to make one complete pivot, so when we enter 2048 the engine will make one complete turn clockwise way by making 2048 stages. To pivot in hostile to clockwise simply enter the number with "– "negative sign. Thus, entering - 1024 will make the engine to pivot a wide portion of the route in hostile to clock shrewd heading. You can enter any ideal qualities, such as entering 1 will make the engine to make just one stride.

Expectation you comprehended the venture and delighted in building it.

Code

// Arduino stepper motor control code

```
#include <Stepper.h> // Include the header file
// change this to the number of steps on your motor
#define STEPS 32
// create an instance of the stepper class using the
steps and pins
Stepper stepper(STEPS, 8, 10, 9, 11);
int val = 0;
void setup() {
 Serial.begin(9600);
 stepper.setSpeed(200);
}
void loop() {
 if (Serial.available()>0)
 {
  val = Serial.parseInt();
  stepper.step(val);
  Serial.println(val); //for debugging
 }

}
```

ARDUINO MOTION DETECTOR UTILIZING PIR SENSOR

Distinguishing movements or developments has consistently been significant in many activities. With

ANBAZHAGAN K

the assistance of the PIR Sensor it turned out to be exceptionally simple to distinguish human/creature developments. In this venture we will figure out how we can interface a PIR Sensor with a microcontroller like Arduino. We will interface an Arduino with PIR module and flicker a LED and signal a Buzzer at whatever point a development is recognized. The accompanying segments will be expected to fabricate this venture.

Materials Required:

- PIR Sensor Module
- LED
- Arduino UNO (any adaptation)
- Breadboard
- Buzzer
- 330 ohm resistor
- Connecting Wires

PIR sensor:

The PIR sensor represents Passive Infrared sensor. It is a minimal effort sensor which can recognize the nearness of Human creatures or creatures. There are two significant materials present in the sensor one is the pyroelectric precious stone which can identify the warmth marks from a living being (people/creatures) and the other is a Fresnel focal points which can augment the scope of the sensor. Likewise the PIR sensor modules give us a few choices to change the working of the sensor as appeared in underneath picture.

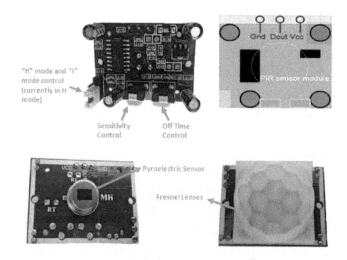

The two potentiometers (orange shading) are utilized to control the affectability and trigger on time of the sensor. Essentially the Dout stick of the sensor is available in the middle of the Vcc and Gnd pins. The module takes a shot at 3.3V yet can be controlled with 5V too. On the upper left corner it likewise has a trigger stick arrangement which can be utilized to make the module work in two unique modes. One is the "H" mode as well as the "I" mode.

In "H" mode the yield stick Dout will go high (3.3V) when an individual is recognized inside range and goes low after a specific (time is set by potentiometer). In this mode the yield stick will go high independent of whether the individual is as yet present inside the range or has left the territory. We are utilizing our module in "H" mode in our undertaking.

In "I" mode the yield stick Dout will go high (3.3V) when an individual is recognized inside range and will remain high as long as he/she remains inside the farthest point of the Sensors go. When the individual has left the territory the stick will go low after the specific time which can be set utilizing the potentiometer.

Note: The situation of potentiometers or pins may fluctuate dependent on your PIR sensor merchant. Pursue the Silk screen to decide you pinouts

Circuit Diagram and Explanation:

The circuit Diagram for arduino movement indicator venture by interfacing Arduino with PIR module and squinting a LED/Buzzer is appeared in the underneath picture.

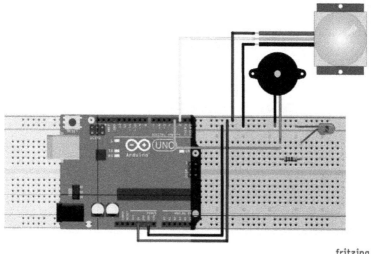

fritzing

We have controlled the PIR sensor utilizing he 5V Rail of the Arduino. The yield stick of the PIR Sensor is combined with the second advanced stick of Arduino. This stick will be the INPUT stick for Arduino. At that point the third stick of Arduino is associated with the LED and Buzzer. This stick will go about as the yield stick of the Arduino. We will program the Arduino to trigger an Output on third stick if an Input has been identified at second stick. The total Program is clarified beneath.

Programming the Arduino:

The program for Arduino is entirely basic and straight forward. To associate Arduino PIR Sensor, we need to allocate the stick number 2 as information and stick number 3 as yield. At that point we need to deliver a broken trigger at whatever point the stick 2 goes high. Each line is clarified beneath.

In the void arrangement capacity demonstrated as follows, we need to proclaim that the stick 2 associated with PIR yield will be utilized as information and the stick 3 associated with LED/Buzzer will be utilized as information.

```
void setup() {

  pinMode(2, INPUT); //Pin 2 as INPUT

  pinMode(3, OUTPUT); //PIN 3 as OUTPUT

}
```

At that point we continue to the circle() work. As we probably am aware the code in here gets executed as long as the MCU is controlled on. So we generally check if the Pin 2 has gone high by utilizing the underneath line inside the circle() work.

```
if (digitalRead(2) == HIGH)
```

On the off chance that we find that the specific stick has gone high, it implies that the PIR module has be activated. In this way, presently we has make our yield (stick 3) to go high. We turn this stick on and off with a postponement of 100 milli second so we can accomplish the blazing or humming yield. The code to do the equivalent is demonstrated as follows.

```
void setup() {

  pinMode(2, INPUT); //Pin 2 as INPUT

  pinMode(3, OUTPUT); //PIN 3 as OUTPUT

}

void loop() {

  if (digitalRead(2) == HIGH) // check if PIR is triggered.

  {

  digitalWrite(3, HIGH);  // turn the LED/Buzz ON

  delay(100);             // wait for 100 msecond

  digitalWrite(3, LOW);  // turn the LED/Buzz OFF

  delay(100);             // wait for 100 msecond
```

```
    }

}
```

Working:

The circuit and program for this arduino movement indicator venture is as of now examined previously. Presently, you can assemble this circuit on a breadboard by following the schematics given above as well as transfer the program found toward the end of this instructional exercise. When your associations are done your set-up should look like something demonstrated as follows.

Presently, control on the Arduino and sit tight for around 50-60 seconds for your PIR sensor to adjust. Try not to be disappointed by the yield that you get during this period. From that point onward, have a go at moving before the PIR sensor and you LED/Buzzer ought to be activated.

The blaring/blazing should stop after some time; you would now be able to toy around the yield by differing the potentiometer to change the affectability or the low time of the module. Expectation you comprehended the undertaking and made it work.

Code

```
void setup() {
 pinMode(2, INPUT); //Pin 2 as INPUT
 pinMode(3, OUTPUT); //PIN 3 as OUTPUT
}
void loop() {
 if (digitalRead(2) == HIGH)
 {
 digitalWrite(3, HIGH);  // turn the LED/Buzz ON
 delay(100);            // wait for 100 msecond
 digitalWrite(3, LOW);  // turn the LED/Buzz OFF
 delay(100);            // wait for 100 msecond
 }
}
```

Thank you !!!